Michigan Wolverines Football Quiz Book

500 Questions on All Things Maize and Blue

Chris Bradshaw

ISBN-13: 978-1-9161230-6-9

Front cover image created by headfuzz by grimboid. Check out his great collection of TV, movie and sport-themed posters online at:

https://www.etsy.com/shop/headfuzzbygrimboid

Introduction

Think you know about Michigan football? Put your knowledge to the test with this collection of quizzes on the Wolverines.

The book covers the whole history of the team, from the early days under Fielding Yost through to the Bo Schembechler era, the 1997 National Champions and the current team under Jim Harbaugh.

The biggest names in school history are present and correct so look out for questions on Desmond Howard, Charles Woodson, Michael Hart, Denard Robinson, Braylon Edwards, Tom Brady and many more.

There are 500 questions in all covering running backs and receivers, coaches and quarterbacks, pass rushers and punters and much else besides.

Each quiz contains a selection of 20 questions and is either a mixed bag of pot luck testers or is centered on a specific category such as receivers or Bowl Games.

There are easy, medium and hard questions offering something for Michigan novices as well as professors of Wolverines history.

You'll find the answers to each quiz below the bottom of the following quiz. For example, the answers to Quiz 1: Pot Luck, are underneath Quiz 2: Quarterbacks. The only exception is Quiz 25: Pot Luck. The answers to these can be found under the Quiz 1 questions.

Statistics are accurate up to the close of the 2019 season.

We hope you enjoy the Michigan Wolverines Football Quiz Book.

About the Author

Chris Bradshaw has written over 30 quiz books including titles for Britain's biggest selling daily newspaper, The Sun, and The Times (of London).

In addition to the NFL, he has written extensively on soccer, cricket, darts and poker.

He lives in Birmingham, England and has been following American sports for over 30 years.

Acknowledgements

Many thanks to Ken and Veronica Bradshaw, Heidi Grant, Steph, James, Ben and Will Roe and Graham Nash.

CONTENTS

Quiz 1: Pot Luck

1. 'AC' was the nickname of which legendary Michigan receiver?

2. The Wolverines are members of which Conference?

3. Who is the only Wolverines receiver with three 1,000-yard seasons?

4. 'Those who stay will be champions' is a phrase associated with which coach?

5. What number jersey did Charles Woodson wear?

6. Who was the first Wolverine to score a touchdown as a rusher, receiver, kick returner and punt returner?

7. In 2008, who became just the second Michigan player to be selected with the first overall pick of the NFL Draft?

8. In what decade did the famous 'Go Blue' banner first appear at Michigan Stadium?

9. Who are the two Michigan head coaches to collect 10 wins in each of their first two seasons in charge?

10. Which Michigan rusher's 87-yard touchdown against the Fighting Irish in 2010 was the longest ever by a visiting player at Notre Dame Stadium?

11. What is the name of the trophy awarded to the winner of the game between Michigan and Michigan State?

12. Which opponent have the Wolverines defeated the most times in their history?

13. Who is the only Michigan player to win the Biletnikoff Award, which is given to the nation's top wide receiver?

14. In what decade did the Wolverines play their first ever night game?

15. Which head coach introduced Michigan's famous winged helmet design?

16. Do the Wolverines have a winning or losing overall record in games against Penn State?

17. Which team selected Michigan's Desmond Howard with the fourth pick of the 1992 NFL Draft?

18. Who was the first African-American to serve as a team captain for the Wolverines?

19. Between 1906 and 1926, Michigan played home games at what venue? a) Farm Field b) Ferry Field c) Flood Field

20. In what year did the Wolverines first play in a televised game? a) 1937 b) 1947 c) 1957

Quiz 25: Answers

1. Alabama 2. Anthony Carter 3. Denard Robinson 4. Chalmers 5. Keith Jackson 6. 70 points 7. Shane Morris 8. True 9. Harris 10. Brandon Herron 11. True 12. Tom Brady 13. Mike Hart 14. 17 points 15. Virginia 16. Scott Dreisbach 17. True 18. 1910s 19. c) Scotland 20. a) Mad Magicians

Quiz 2: Quarterbacks

1. Who is Michigan's all-time leader in passing yards with 9,715?

2. Who is the only other quarterback with more than 9,000 career passing yards?

3. In 2013, who became the first Michigan quarterback to throw for more than 500 yards in a game?

4. Who set a school record in a 2015 game against Indiana after throwing six touchdown passes?

5. Who was the first Michigan quarterback to throw for over 300 yards in a game?

6. In 2019, who became just the third Michigan quarterback to pass for more than 3,000 yards in a single season?

7. Which star of the 1970s has the highest touchdown pass percentage in Wolverines history?

8. In 1991, who became the first Michigan quarterback to toss 25 touchdown passes in a season?

9. Who tied that touchdown pass record in 2004?

10. Who was the first Michigan quarterback with over 200 pass completions in a single season?

11. Who set an unwanted school record at Michigan State in October 1987 after throwing seven interceptions?

12. Of quarterbacks with at least 200 career attempts, who has the lowest interception percentage?

13. Who threw more touchdown passes as a Wolverine – Tom Brady or Brian Griese?

14. Whose 97-yard touchdown pass against Wisconsin in 2007 is the longest in school history?

15. Shea Patterson spent the first two years of his college career with which school?

16. Whose 64.3% completion percentage is the best in school history?

17. Who threw for 368 yards and four touchdowns in his final appearance for Michigan in an overtime win over Alabama in the Orange Bowl on New Year's Day 2000?

18. Who holds the record for throwing the most career interceptions in school history with 39?

19. Who is Michigan's all-time leader in career touchdown passes? a) Tom Brady b) Chad Henne c) John Navarre

20. How many passes did he throw to set that touchdown record? a) 77 b) 82 c) 87

Quiz 1: Answers

1. Anthony Carter 2. Big Ten 3. Braylon Edwards 4. Bo Schembechler 5. #2 6. Desmond Howard 7. Jake Long 8. 1960s 9. Fielding Yost and Jim Harbaugh 10. Denard Robinson 11. The Paul Bunyan – Governor of Michigan Trophy 12. Minnesota 13. Braylon Edwards 14. 1940s 15. Fritz Crisler 16. Winning 17. Washington 18. Ron Johnson 19. b) Ferry Field 20. b) 1947

Quiz 3: Pot Luck

1. What is the name of Michigan's famous fight song?

2. Who holds the school record for the most passing attempts in a single game with 56?

3. Bo Schembechler is one of two Michigan coaches to record double-digit Bowl Game wins. Who is the other?

4. 'Shoelace' was the nickname of which Michigan star?

5. Which Michigan defender was co-winner of the 2009 Big Ten MVP Award?

6. Which Michigan quarterback was drafted by the New York Yankees with the 97th overall pick of the 1998 MLB Draft?

7. The annual award given to Michigan's Most Valuable Player is named after which coach?

8. Which head coach was in charge of the Michigan teams nicknamed the 'Point-A-Minute' squads?

9. Who was Michigan's first African-American starting quarterback?

10. True or false – Michigan has won more Big Ten titles than any other school?

11. Do the Wolverines have a winning or losing all-time record in games against Michigan State?

12. Why did the 2011 game between Michigan and Western Michigan finish in the latter stages of the third quarter?

13. Who had more career receiving yards at Michigan – Jason Avant or Mario Manningham?

14. Which team has defeated Michigan the most times in school history?

15. Who holds the record for the most passing yards in a single season with 3,331?

16. Which Wolverine was the first player in the history of the NCAA to score 23 touchdowns in a single season?

17. Which freshman linebacker registered 16 tackles in a dominant 1988 display against Ohio State?

18. What is former offensive lineman Bubba Paris's real first name?

19. The trophy given to the Big Ten MVP is the 'Chicago Tribune...'? a) Bronze Football b) Silver Football c) Gold Football

20. The longest winning streak in team history ran for how many games? a) 27 b) 28 c) 29

Quiz 2: Answers

1. Chad Henne 2. John Navarre 3. Devin Gardner 4. Jake Ruddock 5. Jim Harbaugh 6. Shea Patterson 7. Rick Leach 8. Elvis Grbac 9. Chad Henne 10. Tom Brady 11. Demetrius Brown 12. Drew Henson 13. Tom Brady 14. Ryan Mallett 15. Ole Miss 16. Todd Collins 17. Tom Brady 18. Denard Robinson 19. a) Chad Henne 20. c) 87

Quiz 4: Running Backs

1. Who is Michigan's all-time leading rusher with 5,040 yards?

2. Whose 1,818 rushing yards are the most by a Michigan back in a single season?

3. In 2003, who won the Doak Walker Award given to the nation's top running back?

4. 'A-Train' was the nickname of which Michigan running back?

5. Who holds the school record for the most 100-yard rushing games in a single season?

6. Whose 92-yard touchdown run against Wisconsin on November 3, 1979 is the longest in school history?

7. Who holds the school record for the most rushing touchdowns in a single season with 19?

8. In a 1995 game against Ohio State, who became just the second Michigan back to rush for more than 300 yards in a game?

9. Which Michigan back caused controversy after referring to the Michigan State Spartans as 'little brother'?

10. Which Wolverine was the first running back to score rushing touchdowns in both the Rose Bowl and the Super Bowl?

11. Which freshman rushed for 726 yards and 11 touchdowns during the 2019 season?

12. Who holds the record for the most rushing yards by a Michigan freshman?

13. Which running back was named the MVP of the Citrus Bowl in both 1999 and 2001?

14. Who is the only Michigan back with three 200-yard rushing games in a single season?

15. Who carried a record 51 times in a 2003 game against Michigan State?

16. Whose 347 rushing yards against Wisconsin on November 16, 1968 are the most in a single game by a Wolverine?

17. Of backs with at least 200 career carries, who has the best yards per rush average?

18. Which back rushed for 236 yards and three touchdowns in the 1988 Hall of Fame Bowl?

19. Who holds the record for the most career rushing touchdowns for the Wolverines? a) Mike Hart b) Denard Robinson c) Anthony Thomas

20. How many touchdowns did he score to set that record? a) 45 b) 55 c) 65

Quiz 3: Answers

1. 'The Victors' 2. Tom Brady 3. Lloyd Carr 4. Denard Robinson 5. Brandon Graham 6. Drew Henson 7. Bo Schembechler 8. Fielding Yost 9. Dennis Franklin 10. True 11. Winning 12. A severe lightning storm struck 13. Mario Manningham 14. Ohio State 15. John Navarre 16. Desmond Howard 17. Erick Anderson 18. William 19. b) Silver Football 20. c) 29 games

Quiz 5: Pot Luck

1. Which opponent do the Wolverines face in the contest known simply as 'The Game'?

2. Which Super Bowl-winning receiver caught a record long 97-yard touchdown pass against Wisconsin in 2007?

3. In what decade did the Wolverines wear their famous winged helmet for the first time?

4. Which coach has steered the Wolverines to the most victories in school history?

5. Which Wolverines defensive back was inducted into the Pro Football Hall of Fame in August 2019?

6. Which Michigan star was the first receiver to win the Big Ten MVP Award?

7. Which quarterback helped the Wolverines overturn a 21-point deficit to give Michigan a famous 2003 win over Minnesota?

8. In 2011, which Michigan lineman won the Rimington Award given to the country's top collegiate center?

9. True or false – Throughout their history, the Wolverines have scored more than 32,000 points?

10. Which Michigan freshman caught a touchdown pass as time expired to inflict the only defeat on Penn State during the 2005 season?

11. Which quarterback threw that famous pass?

12. Do the Wolverines have a winning or losing record in games that have gone to overtime?

13. In the 2017 season opener, the Wolverines wore what color jerseys for the first time since 1928?

14. Who is the only man to act as Michigan's interim head coach? (he later got the job permanently)

15. The annual award given to "the senior football player who demonstrates the most enthusiasm and love for the University of Michigan" is named after which long-time broadcaster?

16. In what year did the Wolverines use a striped ball for the first time?

17. Between 2004 and 2019, how many times did Michigan defeat Ohio State?

18. True or false – More players have been taken from Michigan than from any other school in the history of the NFL Draft?

19. In a 1975 game against Northwestern, Michigan set a school record after rushing for how many yards? a) 553 yards b) 563 yards c) 573 yards

20. Up to the start of the 2020 season the Wolverines had had how many head coaches in team history? a) 17 b) 18 c) 19

Quiz 4: Answers

1. Mike Hart 2. Tim Biakabutuka 3. Chris Perry 4. Anthony Thomas 5. Jamie Morris 6. Butch Woolfolk 7. Ron Johnson 8. Tim Biakabutuka 9. Mike Hart 10. Rob Lytle 11. Zach Charbonnet 12. Mike Hart 13. Anthony Thomas 14. Mike Hart 15. Chris Perry 16. Ron Johnson 17. Jon Vaughn 18. Jamie Morris 19. c) Anthony Thomas 20. b) 55 touchdowns

Quiz 6: Receivers

1. Who is Michigan's all-time leader in receptions with 252?

2. Who holds the school record for the most receiving yards in a single season with 1,373?

3. In 2001, who set a Michigan record after catching 15 passes in a single game, the most in school history?

4. Who was the first Michigan receiver to break the 1,000-yard barrier in back-to-back seasons?

5. Who set a Big Ten record in an October 2013 game against Indiana after amassing 369 receiving yards?

6. In 2007, who became the first Wolverine with over 100 receiving yards in six consecutive games?

7. Who are the two Michigan receivers with over 3,000 career receiving yards?

8. Who tied a school record in a 2015 game against Indiana after catching four touchdown passes?

9. Whose 19 touchdown receptions in 1991 are the most in a single season in school history?

10. Who holds the school record for the most career receptions by a Michigan running back?

11. Who holds the record for the most career receptions and receiving yards by a Michigan tight end?

12. In a November 6, 2010 game against Illinois, which alliteratively named receiver became the first Wolverine with 200 receiving yards in a single game?

13. Who holds the school record for the most career touchdown receptions with 39?

14. Who was the first Michigan player with two 100-yard games in his freshman season? The second coming in a Bowl Game.

15. Whose 15 touchdown receptions between 1995 and 1998 are the most by a Wolverines tight end?

16. Of players with at least 50 career receptions, who has the best yards per catch average?

17. Across the 1990 and 1991 seasons Desmond Howard set a school record after catching a touchdown pass in how many straight games?

18. Who caught a 16-yard touchdown in the final seconds of a 2011 game against Notre Dame to give the Wolverines a famous victory?

19. Who holds the school record for the most consecutive games with at least one reception? a) Anthony Carter b) Braylon Edwards c) Jeremy Gallon

20. That receptions streak ran to how many games? a) 37 b) 38 c) 39

Quiz 5: Answers

1. Ohio State 2. Mario Manningham 3. 1930s 4. Bo Schembechler 5. Ty Law 6. Anthony Carter 7. John Navarre 8. David Molk 9. True 10. Mario Manningham 11. Chad Henne 12. Winning 13. Maize 14. Lloyd Carr 15. Robert P. Ufer 16. 1975 17. Once 18. False 19. c) 573 yards 20. b) 18

Quiz 7: Pot Luck

1. What are the official colors of the Wolverines?

2. In 2010, which Wolverine became the first player in NCAA history with 1,500 rushing and passing yards in the same season?

3. In the first Bowl Game in college football history Michigan defeated which opponent?

4. In what year did that inaugural Bowl Game take place?

5. Which head coach reached 20 wins in the fewest number of games?

6. In 2006, who became the first Michigan player to win the Lombardi Award given to college football's best lineman or linebacker?

7. Who holds the record for the most all-purpose yards in Michigan's history after amassing 6,201 between 1984 and 1987?

8. Before taking the reins at Michigan, Rich Rodriguez had been the head coach at which college?

9. True or false – Former receiver Roy Roundtree is the son of actor Richard Roundtree, best known for playing the private detective 'Shaft'?

10. The Hugh H. Rader Memorial Award is given to the best player in which position group?

11. Do the Wolverines have a winning or losing record in televised games?

12. In October 2004, the Wolverines famously overturned a 27-10 deficit with just 8.43 left to defeat which rival?

13. Who caught a touchdown pass in triple overtime to give the Wolverines that famous 45-37 win?

14. Which quarterback tossed the game-winning pass in that celebrated 2004 victory?

15. True or false – No team in the history of college football has enjoyed as many winning seasons as the Wolverines?

16. Who was the last head coach to steer Michigan to the Big Ten title?

17. In 2012, the Wolverines became the first team to record 900 wins after defeating which rival?

18. Games between Michigan and Ohio State traditionally start at what time?

19. How many Michigan players were selected in the 2020 NFL Draft? a) six b) eight c) ten

20. In what country was running back Tim Biakabutuka born? a) Zaire b) Zambia c) Zimbabwe

Quiz 6: Answers

1. Braylon Edwards 2. Jeremy Gallon 3. Marquise Walker 4. David Terrell 5. Jeremy Gallon 6. Mario Manningham 7. Braylon Edwards and Anthony Carter 8. Jehu Chesson 9. Desmond Howard 10. Jamie Morris 11. Jake Butt 12. Roy Roundtree 13. Braylon Edwards 14. Anthony Carter 15. Jerame Tuman 16. John Kolesar 17. 13 games 18. Roy Roundtree 19. c) Jeremy Gallon 20. c) 39 games

Quiz 8: Defense

1. Which linebacker was named the Big Ten Defensive Player of the Year for 2018?

2. Which linebacker set a school record in a November 2017 game against Minnesota after recording eight tackles for a loss?

3. Which All-American's 25 interceptions between 1967 and 1969 are the most in Michigan's history?

4. Who set a school record after recording five sacks in a 1987 game against Northwestern?

5. Who led the team in tackles for four straight years between 1988 and 1991?

6. Who set a Michigan record in 1996 after recording 12 sacks?

7. Who tied that school sack record in 2006?

8. Which All-American defensive back returned a fumble 83 yards for a touchdown in a 2005 game against Northwestern?

9. Who tied that 83-yard fumble return record in an October 2011 game against Minnesota?

10. Since 1970, which linebacker holds the school record for the most career tackles?

11. Which linebacker and future two-time Super Bowl winner was named the Big Ten Defensive Player of the Year for 2001?

12. Which lineman was named the Chevrolet Defensive Player of the Year for 2006?

13. Which linebacker set a school record against West Michigan in September 2011 after returning an interception 94 yards for a touchdown?

14. Who is the only Michigan player to have won the Butkus Award which is given to the country's top linebacker?

15. Whose 29.5 sacks between 2006 and 2009 are the most by a Michigan player this century?

16. In 2018, which defensive back became just the second player in school history to score two interception return touchdowns in the same season?

17. Which All-American defensive back tied a school record after breaking up 6 passes in an October 2015 game against Michigan State?

18. Who is the only Michigan player to win the Jim Thorpe Award which is given to the nation's top defensive back?

19. Which of the following three Wolverines recorded the most sacks? a) Taco Charlton b) Chase Winovich c) Chris Womley

20. What was All-American safety Tripp Welborne's given first name? a) Salaman b) Solomon c) Sullivan

Quiz 7: Answers

1. Maize and blue 2. Denard Robinson 3. Stanford 4. 1902 5. Fielding Yost 6. LaMarr Woodley 7. Jamie Morris 8. West Virginia 9. False 10. Offensive line 11. Winning 12. Michigan State 13. Braylon Edwards 14. Chad Henne 15. True 16. Lloyd Carr 17. Michigan State 18. Noon 19. c) Ten 20. a) Zaire

Quiz 9: Pot Luck

1. Which future President of the United States played for the Wolverines in the 1930s?

2. What color are the numbers on Michigan's home jersey?

3. Who was the first Wolverine to gain All-American honors three times? (clue: he later became head coach)

4. Which Michigan lineman from the late 1960s early 1970s later became the color analyst on NFL 'Monday Night Football' broadcasts?

5. In 2016, which Wolverine won the Mackey Award which goes to the nation's top tight end?

6. Which Michigan receiver enjoyed a 13-year career in the NFL with the New York Giants, amassing over 9,000 receiving yards between 1996 and 2008?

7. Which versatile Wolverine rushed for 4,495 yards between 2009 and 2012?

8. True or false – In the 1901 season, Michigan outscored their opponents by a combined score of 555-0?

9. What is the highest number of losses the Wolverines have suffered in a single season?

10. Which Michigan running back also won All-American honors on the track in the 110 meters hurdles?

11. In 2004, who became the first Wolverine to win the Rimington Trophy which is given to the nation's top college center?

12. Do the Wolverines have a winning or losing all-time record in games against Ohio State?

13. Which running back won the 2003 Big Ten MVP Award?

14. Which Michigan teammate won the same award a year later in 2004?

15. The Roger Zatkoff Award is given annually to the best Michigan player at which position?

16. Who are the three Michigan backs with more than 800 career carries?

17. Immediately prior to becoming the Michigan head coach, Brady Hoke had been in charge at which college?

18. True or false – The Wolverines have appeared in more televised game than any other college football team?

19. What was the nickname of 1940s halfback Elroy Hirsch? a) Crazy Legs b) Big Bird c) Road Runner

20. What was the name of the 1990s Michigan receiver? a) Jupiter Hayes b) Mars Hayes c) Mercury Hayes

Quiz 8: Answers

1. Devin Bush 2. Khaleke Hudson 3. Tom Curtis 4. Mark Messner 5. Erick Anderson 6. David Bowens 7. LaMarr Woodley 8. Leon Hall 9. Courtney Avery 10. Ron Simpkins 11. Larry Foote 12. LaMarr Woodley 13. Brandon Herron 14. Erick Anderson 15. Brandon Graham 16. Brandon Watson 17. Jourdan Lewis 18. Charles Woodson 19. a) Taco Charlton 20. c) Sullivan

Quiz 10: Special Teams

1. Who set a school record in a November 2018 game against Indiana after converting six field goals?

2. Who holds the record for the most combined kick and punt return touchdowns in school history, scoring five times between 2003 and 2006?

3. Whose 64 successful field goals between 2003 and 2006 are the most in Michigan's history?

4. The longest punt return in school history was a famous 93-yarder against Ohio State in 1991 by which legendary Wolverine?

5. Who holds the record for the most punts in school history with 252?

6. Who is the only player in school history to have returned more than one kickoff for a touchdown?

7. Who returned the opening kickoff 97 yards for a score to give the Wolverines an explosive start to their November 2018 game at Maryland?

8. How long is the longest punt in school history?

9. Who has been Michigan's most accurate field goal kicker this century, converting 82.2% of his attempts between 2013 and 2016?

10. Who successfully converted a school record 16 field goals in a row across the 2012 and 2013 seasons?

11. Who returned a kickoff 99 yards for a touchdown at Notre Dame on September 1, 2018?

12. Who set a school record in 2018 after averaging 46.98 yards per punt?

13. Which alliteratively named player scored the longest kick return touchdown in Michigan's history, taking it 100 yards for a score against Wisconsin in 1984?

14. True or false – The most times the Wolverines have punted in a single game is 24?

15. Who kicked the game-winning field goal to give the Wolverines a 34-31 overtime win over Michigan State in 2005?

16. In 1994, who set the school record for the most successful field goals in a season after converting 25 kicks?

17. Which future NFL kicker converted a record 10 extra points in a 1981 game against Illinois?

18. In which east European country was former punter Zoltan Mesko born?

19. How long is the longest successful field goal in Michigan's history? a) 56 yards b) 57 yards c) 58 yards

20. Who booted that record-setting field goal against Michigan State in November 2001? a) Hayden Epstein b) Jay Feely c) Remy Hamilton

Quiz 9: Answers

1. Gerald Ford 2. Maize 3. Bennie Oosterbaan 4. Dan Dierdorf 5. Jake Butt 6. Amani Toomer 7. Denard Robinson 8. True 9. Nine 10. Tyrone Wheatley 11. David Baas 12. Winning 13. Chris Perry 14. Braylon Edwards 15. Linebacker 16. Mike Hart, Anthony Thomas and Jamie Morris 17. Oregon State 18. True 19. a) Crazy Legs 20. c) Mercury Hayes

Quiz 11: Pot Luck

1. Which Wolverine won the Heisman Trophy in 1997?

2. Who combined for 584 passing and rushing yards against Indiana in 2013, the most in school history?

3. Before becoming the head coach at Michigan, Bo Schembechler had a spell as the head coach of what other college?

4. Which defensive superstar famously returned a fumble 56 yards for a touchdown in a September 2006 game at Notre Dame?

5. Who tied Michigan's longest field goal in the 2020 Citrus Bowl?

6. True or false – Former star Wolverines offensive lineman Jake Long is the son of NFL Hall of Famer Howie Long?

7. Does Michigan have a winning or losing all-time record in games against Notre Dame?

8. Which Michigan coach was journalist Grantland Rice describing when he wrote, "No other man has ever given as much heart, soul, brains, and tongue to the game he loved—football"?

9. Who was the last Wolverines quarterback to lead the team to a Big Ten championship?

10. Which running back caught 44 passes in 2003, the most ever by a Michigan rusher in a single season?

11. Who was the only Michigan quarterback to win the Big Ten MVP Award during the 1970s?

12. In what decade was a Michigan game broadcast on the radio for the first time?

13. True or false – Mike Hart never lost a fumble during his time with the Wolverines?

14. Which Wolverine appeared on the cover of the video game NCAA Football 14?

15. What number jersey did Desmond Howard wear?

16. Former Michigan receiver Amara Darboh was born in which west African country?

17. Which former Wolverine is the only special teamer to have won the Super Bowl MVP Award?

18. True or false – The Wolverines have never lost a night game at Michigan Stadium?

19. What was the nickname of College Hall of Fame member John Maulbetsch? a) The Human Bullet b) The Human Cannon c) The Human Missile

20. Up to 2019, the Wolverines had recorded how many unbeaten seasons? a) 22 b) 23 c) 24

Quiz 10: Answers

1. Jake Moody 2. Steve Breaston 3. Garrett Rivas 4. Desmond Howard 5. Zoltan Mesko 6. Desmond Howard 7. Giles Jackson 8. 82 yards 9. Kenny Allen 10. Brendan Gibbons 11. Ambry Thomas 12. Will Hart 13. Seth Smith 14. True 15. Garrett Rivas 16. Remy Hamilton 17. Ali Haji-Sheikh 18. Romania 19. b) 57 yards 20. a) Hayden Epstein

Quiz 12: 1997 National Champions

1. Who was the head coach of the Wolverines team that won the 1997 National Championship?

2. Which opponent did the Wolverines defeat in the Rose Bowl?

3. Who was named the Player of the Game in that Rose Bowl triumph?

4. Who was Michigan's leading rusher during the 1997 season?

5. Which receiver led the team in 1997 with 476 yards?

6. The Wolverines opened the season with a 27-3 win over which opponent who had previously enjoyed a famous win in Ann Arbor?

7. Who caught a pair of touchdown passes in the Rose Bowl triumph?

8. Who led the Wolverines with eight interceptions in 1997?

9. U-M topped the AP National Poll but which school beat the Wolverines to top spot in the USA Today Coaches' Poll?

10. Prior to 1997, in what year had Michigan last claimed a National Championship?

11. Who were the two captains of the 1997 team?

12. Who was the only Wolverines defender to intercept two passes in a game twice during the 1997 season?

13. Who returned a punt for a touchdown, intercepted a pass and had a 37-yard reception during the 20-14 win over Ohio State?

14. Whose 129 yards rushing against Iowa was the best by a Michigan player during the 1997 season?

15. Who was the offensive coordinator of the 1997 Wolverines team?

16. Who was the defensive coordinator of the 1997 team?

17. The Wolverines recorded a single shutout in 1997, defeating which team by a score of 37-0 on October 4?

18. Jay Feely and which other kicker converted field goals during the 1997 season?

19. The Wolverines restricted their opponents to how many points during the 1997 season? a) 114 b) 124 c) 134

20. How many of Michigan's 1997 roster went on to play in the NFL? a) 11 b) 21 c) 31

Quiz 11: Answers

1. Charles Woodson 2. Devin Gardner 3. Miami (Ohio) 4. LaMarr Woodley 5. Quinn Nordin 6. False 7. Winning 8. Fielding Yost 9. Chad Henne 10. Chris Perry 11. Rick Leach 12. 1920s 13. False 14. Denard Robinson 15. #21 16. Sierra Leone 17. Desmond Howard 18. False 19. a) The Human Bullet 20. b) 23 seasons

Quiz 13: Pot Luck

1. Which Michigan star won the 1991 Heisman Trophy?

2. What color are the numbers on Michigan's road jersey?

3. Who is Michigan's all-time leader in forced fumbles?

4. Who are the two Wolverines with more than 2,000 all-purpose yards in a single season?

5. What is the name of the trophy awarded to the winner of games played between Michigan and the Minnesota Golden Gophers?

6. Who was the only Michigan quarterback to win the Big Ten MVP Award during the 1980s?

7. In which round of the 2000 NFL Draft did the New England Patriots select Michigan quarterback Tom Brady?

8. Which former Wolverine was the first running back for the NFL's New York Giants to rush for over 1,000 yards in a season?

9. Who was the first Wolverine with over 500 combined rushing and passing yards in a single game?

10. Which head coach has steered the Wolverines to the most Bowl Game victories?

11. Which team defeated the Wolverines in the game known as the 'Miracle at Michigan'?

12. What number uniform did Tom Brady wear while a Wolverine?

13. The Dick Katcher Award is given to the best Michigan player in which position group?

14. Who is the only Michigan defender to have been selected among the top 5 overall picks of the NFL Draft?

15. Since its foundation in 2011, who are the two Wolverines to have won the Kwalick–Clark Award given to the Big Ten's top tight end?

16. In what year did the Wolverines play their first night game at Michigan Stadium?

17. Which opponent did the team face in that historic, floodlit encounter?

18. Who caught a 20-yard touchdown pass on a 4th and 3 play in the closing stages of the 1988 Hall of Fame Bowl to give Michigan a 28-24 win over Alabama?

19. What was Bo Schembechler's given first name? a) Gary b) Glenn c) Grady

20. Up to the close of the 2019 season the Wolverines had won how many Conference championships? a) 40 b) 41 c) 42

Quiz 12: Answers

1. Lloyd Carr 2. Washington State 3. Brian Griese 4. Chris Howard 5. Tai Streets 6. Colorado 7. Tai Streets 8. Charles Woodson 9. Nebraska 10. 1948 11. Jon Jansen and Eric Mayes 12. Marcus Ray 13. Charles Woodson 14. Anthony Thomas 15. Mike DeBord 16. Jim Herrmann 17. Indiana 18. Kraig Baker 19. a) 114 20. c) 31

Quiz 14: Wolverines in the NFL

1. Who was the first player in NFL history to be named the Super Bowl MVP four times?

2. Who succeeded John Elway as the Denver Broncos' starting quarterback?

3. Who started and ended his NFL career with the Raiders but won a Super Bowl with the Packers in between?

4. Who was a member of the Michigan Panthers team that won the first USFL Championship then later enjoyed great success in the NFL with Minnesota and later Detroit?

5. Who was drafted by the Browns in the first round in 2005 and later had spells with the Jets (twice), 49ers and Seahawks?

6. Drafted by Miami, which legendary lineman went to the Pro Bowl in three straight seasons in 2009, 2010 and 2011?

7. Which linebacker won a Super Bowl ring in his second season with the Pittsburgh Steelers and later had spells with Oakland and Arizona?

8. Who caught a crucial 38-yard pass with less than 4 minutes remaining in Super Bowl XLVI to help give the Giants the win over New England?

9. Who recorded a strip-sack in the closing stages of Super Bowl LII to seal victory for Philadelphia over the Patriots?

10. Which former Wolverine rushed for 62 and 67-yard touchdowns in a 1999 game for the Carolina Panthers against the Cincinnati Bengals?

11. Which quarterback won a Super Bowl ring as a backup with the 49ers before becoming a starter in Kansas City and later, Baltimore?

12. Which speedy returner and receiver caught 255 passes for the Cardinals and Chiefs between 2007 and 2012?

13. Drafted by Miami in 2008, who was the third-string quarterback on the Kansas City Chiefs team that won Super Bowl LIV?

14. Which former Michigan defender recorded five sacks during the postseason in Kansas City's Super Bowl LIV-winning run?

15. Which former Wolverines QB started a game for the Buffalo Bills in Dec 1997 then had to wait over 10 years for his next start, this time for Washington?

16. Drafted by the Bengals in 2007, which defensive back also played for the Giants, 49ers and Raiders, registering 27 picks and three TDs?

17. Which kicker appeared in 211 games for six different teams in an NFL career that ran from 2001 through to 2014?

18. Which linebacker, who won two Super Bowl rings with the Steelers in the 2000s, was appointed an assistant coach with the Bucs in 2019?

19. Which former Michigan defensive back led the NFL with nine interceptions in 1981 to help the 49ers to their first Super Bowl triumph?

20. Which dominant offensive lineman from 1978 to 1981, later won three Super Bowls with the 49ers?

Quiz 13: Answers

1. Desmond Howard 2. Blue 3. LaMarr Woodley 4. Chris Perry & Anthony Thomas 5. The Little Brown Jug 6. Jim Harbaugh 7. 6th 8. Ron Johnson 9. Denard Robinson 10. Lloyd Carr 11. Colorado 12. #10 13. Defensive linemen 14. Charles Woodson 15. Jake Butt & Devin Funchess 16. 2011 17. Notre Dame 18. John Kolesar 19. b) Glenn 20. c) 42

Quiz 15: Pot Luck

1. In 1940, who became the first Wolverine to win the Heisman Trophy?

2. Who holds the school record for the most combined passing and rushing yards in school history?

3. Who has been Michigan's leading scorer this century, amassing 354 points between 2003 and 2006?

4. Which Michigan alumnus was named 2001 NFL Rookie of the Year?

5. Whose spectacular catch and run for a 45-yard touchdown as time expired gave the Wolverines a famous 27-21 win over Indiana in 1979?

6. Which quarterback threw that game-winning touchdown pass?

7. In 2009, who became the first Wolverines punter to be elected a team captain?

8. True or false – The Wolverines had a winning regular season record in each year of Bo Schembechler's tenure as head coach?

9. What number jersey did Brian Griese wear while a Wolverine?

10. Which Wolverines great later went on to become a successful wine producer, creating the label Intercept Wines?

11. Who holds the record for the most career receiving yards by a Wolverines running back?

12. Did the Wolverines have a winning or losing record in the series known as 'The Ten Year War'?

13. Which two Michigan defensive stars were chosen by the Steelers and Packers with the 10th and 12th overall picks of the 2019 NFL Draft?

14. Who is the regular play-by-play announcer on Wolverines radio broadcasts?

15. Which former Michigan running back was the subject of a documentary called 'Perseverance'?

16. True or false – A Michigan player has been selected in the NFL Draft every year since its inception?

17. Who are the two Michigan players to have won the Walter Camp Player of the Year Award?

18. Which pair of Michigan backs combined for 391 rushing yards against Minnesota in in November 2017?

19. In what year did Michigan play their first intercollegiate football game? a) 1879 b) 1889 c) 1899

20. Which opponent did Michigan face in that inaugural game? a) Notre Dame b) Ohio State c) Racine College

Quiz 14: Answers

1. Tom Brady 2. Brian Griese 3. Charles Woodson 4. Anthony Carter 5. Braylon Edwards 6. Jake Long 7. LaMarr Woodley 8. Mario Manningham 9. Brandon Graham 10. Tim Biakabutuka 11. Elvis Grbac 12. Steve Breaston 13. Chad Henne 14. Frank Clark 15. Todd Collins 16. Leon Hall 17. Jay Feely 18. Larry Foote 19. Dwight Hicks 20. Bubba Paris

Quiz 16: Michigan Stadium

1. Michigan Stadium is sometimes known as 'The Big...'?

2. True or false – Michigan Stadium is the largest football stadium in America?

3. In what year did the Wolverines play their first game at Michigan Stadium?

4. Which opponent did Michigan face in that first game at the stadium?

5. Is the field at Michigan Stadium made of natural grass or artificial turf?

6. In 2013, Michigan set the record for the best attended game in football history. To the nearest thousand, how many were at the game?

7. Which opponent did Michigan defeat 41-30 in that record-breaking contest?

8. In 2018, the end zones at Michigan Stadium were painted what color for the first time?

9. In what decade did Michigan Stadium host its first crowd of over 100,000?

10. True or false – The land on which Michigan Stadium was built was originally a farm?

11. In what year did the Wolverines start their streak of games with an attendance of at least 100,000?

12. The 2008 Wolverines tied an unwanted school record after losing how many successive games at Michigan Stadium?

13. At the close of the 2019 season, what was the official capacity of Michigan Stadium?

14. Which team did the Wolverines defeat by a score of 67-65 in 2010, making it the highest scoring game ever played at Michigan Stadium?

15. Who is the only player to have scored five touchdowns in a single game at Michigan Stadium?

16. True or false – Michigan Stadium was the first venue to use electronic scoreboards to run the official game clock?

17. All Michigan Stadium capacity numbers end with the digit '1' to honor which former athletic director?

18. The longest unbeaten run at Michigan Stadium stretched from 1969 through to 1975 and ran for how many games?

19. How much did Michigan Stadium cost to build? a) $95,000 b) $950,000 c) $9.5 million

20. According to legend, what is buried underneath Michigan Stadium? a) a crane b) a dumper truck c) a steam roller

Quiz 15: Answers

1. Tom Harmon 2. Denard Robinson 3. Garrett Rivas 4. Anthony Thomas 5. Anthony Carter 6. John Wangler 7. Zoltan Mesko 8. False – There was a 6-6 season in 1984 9. #14 10. Charles Woodson 11. Anthony Thomas 12. Winning 13. Devin Bush and Rashan Gary 14. Jim Brandstatter 15. Billy Taylor 16. True 17. Desmond Howard and Charles Woodson 18. Karan Higdon and Chris Evans 19. a) 1879 20. c) Racine College

Quiz 17: Pot Luck

1. The University of Michigan is based in which town?

2. In 2019, which wide receiver became just the second player in school history to score rushing, receiving and kick return touchdowns in his freshman season?

3. Who was the last player to achieve that freshman scoring hat-trick? (clue: it was in 1972)

4. In 1985, who set a school record after catching eight touchdown passes, the most in a season by a Michigan tight end?

5. Michigan has played road games in front of crowds of over 110,000 against which two opponents?

6. Which Wolverine was named the 2010 Big Ten MVP?

7. 'Rock' was the nickname of which dominant offensive lineman from the 1990s?

8. Which quarterback had a starting record of 30-2-1 during his time with the Wolverines in the early 1970s?

9. True or false – The Wolverines have never lost a game in which they've had two rushers pass the 100-yard mark?

10. Which quarterback finished third in the Heisman Trophy vote in 1986?

11. Who is the only Michigan running back with over 1,000 career carries?

12. True or false – In the 2011 season, the Wolverines wore special white jerseys with zebra-style maize and blue striped sleeves?

13. Which Michigan running back was selected by Chicago with the first pick of the 1941 NFL Draft but never played a game for the Bears?

14. Michigan overturned 14-0 and 28-14 deficits before going on to beat which team 35-34 in the Orange Bowl on New Year's Day 2000?

15. With 10 receptions for 150 yards and three touchdowns, who was the MVP of that famous Orange Bowl triumph?

16. Who was the first Wolverine to appear on the cover of the NCAA Football video game? (clue it was 1999)

17. Which backup quarterback threw a 69-yard touchdown pass as Michigan shocked Ohio State by a score of 13-9 in 1996?

18. Who caught that famous touchdown pass against the Buckeyes?

19. Throughout their history, the Wolverines have played competitive games against how many different opponents? a) 85 b) 95 c) 105

20. In a 1971 game against Minnesota, the Wolverines set a school record after rushing how many times? a) 75 b) 85 c) 95

Quiz 16: Answers

1. House 2. True 3. 1927 4. Ohio Wesleyan 5. Artificial turf 6. 115,109 7. Notre Dame 8. Blue 9. 1950s 10. True 11. 1975 12. Five 13. 107,601 14. Illinois 15. Ron Johnson 16. True 17. Fritz Crisler 18. 41 games 19. b) $950,000 20. a) A crane

Quiz 18: Jim Harbaugh

1. Harbaugh's first season as Michigan head coach was in what year?

2. How many regular season games did the Wolverines win in Harbaugh's first season in charge?

3. Whom did Harbaugh succeed as Michigan head coach?

4. Michigan closed out Harbaugh's first season in charge by beating which team in the Citrus Bowl?

5. Before taking the reins at Michigan, Harbaugh had been the head coach at which NFL team?

6. While a player, Harbaugh famously guaranteed victory over which opponent in a 1986 encounter?

7. What number jersey did Harbaugh wear while a player with the Wolverines?

8. Who is older – Jim or his brother and fellow head coach, John?

9. Which NFL team drafted Harbaugh in 1987?

10. In which round of the NFL Draft was Harbaugh selected?

11. Harbaugh also had spells as a player with which three AFC teams?

12. Harbaugh started his head coaching career with a spell at which college?

13. Between 2007 and 2010, Harbaugh enjoyed great success as the head coach of which college?

14. Harbaugh was the quarterbacks coach of which AFC team that went to the Super Bowl in the early 2000s?

15. Prior to Harbaugh, who was the last former Michigan player to go on to become the Wolverines head coach?

16. True or false – Harbaugh made a cameo appearance in the TV comedy 'Saved By The Bell'?

17. Complete the name of Harbaugh's NFL nickname – Captain...?

18. True or false – Jim Harbaugh is the only former Michigan player to have gone on to become an NFL head coach?

19. In what state was Harbaugh born? a) California b) Michigan c) Ohio

20. How many touchdown passes did Harbaugh throw in his Michigan career? a) 21 b) 31 c) 41

Quiz 17: Answers

1. Ann Arbor 2. Giles Jackson 3. Gil Chapman 4. Eric Kattus 5. Penn State and Ohio State 6. Denard Robinson 7. Jon Jansen 8. Dennis Franklin 9. False 10. Jim Harbaugh 11. Mike Hart 12. True 13. Tom Harmon 14. Alabama 15. David Terrell 16. Charles Woodson 17. Brian Griese 18. Tai Streets 19. c) 105 20. b) 85

Quiz 19: Pot Luck

1. Up to the start of the 2020 season the Wolverines had won how many National Championships?

2. Who holds the record for the most receiving yards by a Michigan tight end in a single season?

3. Which future NFL star threw a record six interceptions for Miami. Fla in a 1984 game against the Wolverines at Michigan Stadium?

4. In 2004, who became just the second true freshman quarterback in Michigan's history to start a season opener?

5. What number jersey did running back Tim Biakabutuka wear while a Wolverine?

6. In 2007, the Wolverines suffered one of the most infamous defeats in their history, losing 34-32 at home to which FCS school in the season opener?

7. Who is the only Michigan quarterback to have won the Sammy Baugh Trophy which is awarded to the nation's top college passer?

8. True or false – The Wolverines were unbeaten against the Minnesota Golden Gophers in games played at the Hubert H. Humphrey Metrodome?

9. In what decade did numbers first appear on the front of the Wolverines' jerseys?

10. Who led the team in rushing for four straight seasons from 2004 through 2007?

11. The Wolverines started their streak of home games with an attendance of at least 100,000 spectators against which opponent?

12. In 1985, who became the first freshman to record two 100-yard receiving games in the regular season?

13. Which opponent did the Wolverines defeat 38-31 in the Rose Bowl on New Year's Day 1993?

14. Which back rushed for 235 yards and three touchdowns on just 15 carries in that famous Rose Bowl win?

15. The Chicago Bears used the eighth overall pick of the 2001 NFL Draft to select which Michigan receiver?

16. Which was star defender Ty Law's given first name?

17. Who was the first Michigan head coach with five Bowl Game wins?

18. Which Michigan running back finished third in the voting for the Heisman Trophy in 1976?

19. What was Butch Woofolk's given first name? a) Hadrian b) Harold c) Henry

20. Bo Schembechler was the head coach of the Wolverines for how many seasons? a) 19 b) 20 c) 21

Quiz 18: Answers

1. 2015 2. Nine 3. Brady Hoke 4. Florida 5. San Francisco 6. Ohio State 7. #4 8. John 9. Chicago 10. First 11. Indianapolis, Baltimore and San Diego 12. San Diego University 13. Stanford 14. Oakland 15. Bump Elliott 16. True 17. Comeback 18. True 19. c) Ohio 20. b) 31

Quiz 20: Bowl Games

1. Which Bowl Game have the Wolverines appeared in the most times?

2. Does Michigan have a winning or losing record in Bowl Games?

3. Chad Henne holds the Michigan record for the most career touchdown passes in Bowl Games. Who is second on that list?

4. Who became the first Michigan back to rush for 200 yards in a Bowl Game against Alabama on Jan 2, 1988?

5. Michigan routed which school by a score of 41-7 in the 2016 Citrus Bowl?

6. Which back's 88-yard TD run in the 1993 Rose Bowl is the longest by a Michigan rusher in a Bowl Game?

7. Which quarterback holds the record for the most passing yards in a Bowl Game after throwing for 373 in the 2008 Capital One Bowl?

8. True or false – In the 1976 Orange Bowl against Oklahoma, the Wolverines completed just two passes?

9. In Lloyd Carr's last game as head coach on Jan 1, 2008, underdog Michigan defeated which opponent 41-35 in the Capital One Bowl?

10. Who is Michigan's all-time leader in receiving yards in Bowl Games with 395?

11. Michigan's longest winning run in Bowl Games stretched to how many games?

12. Who is the only Michigan receiver to have had 10 or more receptions in a Bowl Game more than once?

13. Which QB's 76-yard TD to Curt Stephenson in the 1978 Rose Bowl is the longest Bowl Game pass thrown by a Wolverine?

14. Which future Denver Broncos linebacker set a school record in the 1999 Citrus Bowl against Arkansas after returning a pick 46 yards for a TD?

15. True or false – Michigan appeared in a Bowl Game for 33 consecutive seasons between the 1975 and 2007?

16. What did Michigan do in the 2018 Peach Bowl that they hadn't done in a Bowl Game since the 1972 Rose Bowl?

17. Which DT, who spent 11 years in the NFL between 2007 and 2017, is the only Wolverine to record three sacks in a single Bowl Game?

18. Which rusher set a school record after scoring four touchdowns in the 2003 Outback Bowl?

19. The Wolverines won both of their first two appearances in the Rose Bowl by what score? a) 29-0 b) 39-0 c) 49-0

20. Up to the start of the 2020 season, the Wolverines had appeared in how many Bowl Games? a) 38 b) 48 c) 58

Quiz 19: Answers

1. Eleven 2. Devin Funchess 3. Bernie Kosar 4. Chad Henne 5. #21 6. Appalachian State 7. Elvis Grbac 8. True 9. 1930s 10. Mike Hart 11. Purdue 12. John Kolesar 13. Washington 14. Tyrone Wheatley 15. David Terrell 16. Tajuan 17. Bo Schembechler 18. Rob Lytle 19. b) Harold 20. c) 21 seasons

Quiz 21: Pot Luck

1. What is the name of quarterback Dylan McCaffrey's dad who won two Super Bowl rings with Denver?

2. Who holds the school record for the most career 100-yard receiving games with 17?

3. Up to and including 2019 season, which two colleges have the Wolverines faced more than 100 times?

4. In 1975, who became the first true freshman quarterback to start a season opener for the Wolverines?

5. Which Michigan offensive line star was hospitalized for smoke inhalation after a fire in a shared house in 2004?

6. Which legendary Wolverines running back returned to Michigan as the team's running back coach in 2015?

7. Who was the first wide receiver to appear on the cover of the NCAA Football video game?

8. Which Michigan head coach was 4-1 in Bowl Games between 1990 and 1994?

9. True or false – In 1992, the Wolverines went unbeaten despite winning just eight regular season games?

10. Which offensive lineman was the only Michigan player picked in the first round of the 2020 NFL Draft?

11. Which team made that 2020 first-round Draft pick?

12. In 1977 and 1978, who became just the second Wolverine to make the top 10 in the Heisman Trophy voting more than once?

13. After leaving Michigan, coach Bo Schembechler had a spell as president of which Major League Baseball team?

14. Who is the only Michigan head coach to have a losing win loss record?

15. True or false – Michigan's largest win over Ohio State was 86-0?

16. Who intercepted three passes and returned a punt 61 yards to set up a touchdown in Michigan's historic 1969 win over #1 ranked Ohio State?

17. Which former Michigan and NFL star has been the color commentator on Wolverines radio broadcasts since 2014?

18. True or false – Legendary 1950s Michigan lineman Ron Kramer was drafted by the NBA's Detroit Pistons?

19. Between 1893 and 1905 Michigan played home game at what venue? a) Kings Field b) Princes Field c) Regents Field

20. In what year did the Wolverines face Ohio State for the first time? a) 1897 b) 1907 c) 1917

Quiz 20: Answers

1. The Rose Bowl 2. Losing 3. Elvis Grbac 4. Jamie Morris 5. Florida 6. Tyrone Wheatley 7. Chad Henne 8. True 9. Florida 10. Anthony Carter 11. Four 12. Braylon Edwards 13. Rick Leach 14. Ian Gold 15. True 16. Score a safety 17. Alan Branch 18. Chris Perry 19. c) 49-0 20. b) 48

Quiz 22: Numbers Game

What number jersey did the following Michigan players wear?

1. John Wangler and Marquise Walker

2. Denard Robinson and John Navarre

3. Jamie Morris and Chris Perry

4. Tai Streets and Mario Manningham

5. Tom Harmon and Devin Gardner

6. Rick Leach and Chad Henne

7. Dwight Hicks and Larry Foote

8. Braylon Edwards and Anthony Carter

9. Elvis Grbac and Steve Breaston

10. Mike Hart and Ian Gold

11. Amani Toomer and Bump Elliott

12. Jake Butt and Derrick Walker

13. Garrett Rivas and Bob Wiese

14. Jerame Tuman and Alan Branch

15. Tripp Welborne and Marlin Jackson

16. Leon Hall and Marcus Ray

17. Jason Avant and Trevor Pryce

18. Gordon Bell and Jabrill Peppers

19. Dan Dierdorf and Jumbo Elliott

20. Rob Lytle and Zoltan Mesko

Quiz 21: Answers

1. Ed 2. Braylon Edwards 3. Minnesota and Ohio State 4. Rick Leach 5. Jake Long 6. Tyrone Wheatley 7. Desmond Howard 8. Gary Moeller 9. True 10. Cesar Ruiz 11. New Orleans 12. Rick Leach 13. Detroit Tigers 14. Rich Rodriguez 15. True 16. Barry Pierson 17. Dan Dierdorf 18. True 19. c) Regents Field 20. a) 1897

Quiz 23: Pot Luck

1. Do the Wolverines have an all-time winning or losing record?

2. Who was the first Michigan coach to lead the team to four successive Bowl Game victories?

3. John Harbaugh is noted for always wearing what color pants while on the sideline?

4. Which true freshman quarterback was 3-0 as a starter in 2007, steering the Wolverines to wins over Notre Dame, Penn State and Minnesota?

5. Who is the only Michigan player to have won the Ted Hendricks Award which is given to college football's top defensive end?

6. During his freshman and sophomore years Tom Brady served as backup to which future NFL quarterback?

7. In 2007, four Michigan defenders were picked within the first 47 picks of the NFL Draft. Name the quartet.

8. True or false – Anthony Carter never enjoyed a 1,000-yard season at Michigan?

9. Who was named MVP of the 1981 Rose Bowl against Washington after rushing for 182 yards?

10. Which former Michigan quarterback played Major League Baseball for the Detroit Tigers, Toronto Blue Jays, Texas Rangers and San Francisco Giants between 1981 and 1990?

11. Bo Schembechler secured his second Rose Bowl victory on January 2, 1989 after the Wolverines defeated which California school?

12. Whose autobiography was titled, 'Doing It My Way: My Outspoken Life as a Michigan Wolverine, NFL Receiver, and Beyond'?

13. True or false – Michigan has provided more players to the NFL Pro Football Hall of Fame than any other college?

14. Michigan staged a famous goal line stand in their first ever game against which opponent in 1993?

15. Who was the first Michigan back to rush for 10 touchdowns in his freshman season?

16. In 1993, the Wolverines routed unbeaten Ohio State by what scoreline?

17. What is the highest number of Michigan players selected in a single NFL Draft?

18. Which Wolverines defensive back from the 1970s later enjoyed a successful career as an actor, appearing in shows including 'E.R.', 'The O.C.' and 'How I Met Your Mother'?

19. The 1950 matchup between Michigan and Ohio State was known as…? a) The Rain Bowl b) The Snow Bowl c) The Wind Bowl

20. The two teams punted how many times in that famous weather affected game? a) 25 b) 35 c) 45

Quiz 22: Answers

1. #4 2. #16 3. #23 4. #86 5. #98 6. #7 7. #17 8. #1 9. #15 10. #20 11. #18 12. #88 13. #38 14. #80 15. #3 16. #29 17. #8 18. #5 19. #72 20. #41

Quiz 24: Anagrams

Rearrange the letter to make the name of a former Michigan man.

1. Modern Dad Show

2. Body Mart

3. Beer Raising

4. Hath Miracle

5. Newly Hot Eatery

6. Borderlands Way

7. Germany Jello

8. Chalk Rice

9. Rowdy Ole Alarm

10. Ranch Attorney

11. Jan Rave Horn

12. Cherry Rips

13. A Snag Harry

14. Ankle Jog

15. Rebel Twin Prop

16. Travel Riddle

17. Lawmaker Squire

18. Eaten Run Jam

19. Royal Forte

20. Dollar Cry

Quiz 23: Answers

1. Winning 2. Lloyd Carr 3. Khaki 4. Ryan Mallett 5. LaMarr Woodley 6. Brian Griese 7. Leon Hall, Alan Branch, LaMarr Woodley, David Harris 8. True 9. Butch Woolfolk 10. Rick Leach 11. USC 12. Braylon Edwards 13. False 14. Penn State 15. Zach Charbonnet 16. 28-0 17. Eleven 18. Dwight Hicks 19. b) The Snow Bowl 20. c) 45 times

Quiz 25: Pot Luck

1. Which team did the Wolverines face in the 2020 Citrus Bowl?

2. In the early 1980s, which wide receiver became just the third Wolverine to receive All-American honors three times?

3. Who holds the Big Ten record for the most rushing yards by a quarterback in a single game?

4. What was coach Bump Elliott's given first name?

5. Which broadcaster is credited with giving Michigan Stadium its nickname of 'The Big House'?

6. What is the most points that the Wolverines have scored in a game at Michigan Stadium?

7. Which left-hander was the last true freshman quarterback to appear for the Wolverines?

8. True or false – Legendary offensive lineman Steve Hutchinson arrived at Michigan as a defensive tackle?

9. What did the H stand for in the name of the legendary Michigan coach Fielding H. Yost?

10. In a 2011 game against WMU, who became the first Wolverine to score interception and fumble return touchdowns in the same game?

11. True or false – Since it opened, more than 50 million spectators have watched Wolverines games at Michigan Stadium?

12. Who was the first Michigan quarterback to pass for over 300 yards in a game three times?

13. Who was the first Wolverine to rush for 1,000 yards in his freshman season?

14. The Wolverines entered the historic 1969 matchup against Ohio State as an underdog by how many points?

15. Michigan overturned a 0-17 deficit to beat which opponent 18-17 in the 1995 season-opening Pigskin Classic?

16. Which freshman quarterback orchestrated that comeback win?

17. True or false – Michigan quarterbacks coach Ben McDaniels is the brother of longtime New England Patriots offensive coordinator Josh McDaniels?

18. In what decade did numbers first appear on the back of the Michigan players' uniforms?

19. Nigerian-born defensive lineman David Ojabo was raised in which country? a) France b) Ireland c) Scotland

20. By what nickname were the all-conquering 1947 Wolverines known? a) Mad Magicians b) Soaraway Sorcerers c) Wild Wizards

Quiz 24: Answers

1. Desmond Howard 2. Tom Brady 3. Brian Griese 4. Michael Hart 5. Tyrone Wheatley 6. Braylon Edwards 7. Jeremy Gallon 8. Rick Leach 9. LaMarr Woodley 10. Anthony Carter 11. John Navarre 12. Chris Perry 13. Rashan Gary 14. Jake Long 15. Tripp Welborne 16. David Terrell 17. Marquise Walker 18. Jerame Tuman 19. Larry Foote 20. Lloyd Carr

Made in United States
North Haven, CT
07 December 2023

45295528R00036